Copyright © Ramya Satheesh
All Rights Reserved.

This book has been self-published with all reasonable efforts taken to make the material error-free by the author. No part of this book shall be used, reproduced in any manner whatsoever without written permission from the author, except in the case of brief quotations embodied in critical articles and reviews.

The Author of this book is solely responsible and liable for its content including but not limited to the views, representations, descriptions, statements, information, opinions, and references ["Content"]. The Content of this book shall not constitute or be construed or deemed to reflect the opinion or expression of the Publisher or Editor. Neither the Publisher nor Editor endorse or approve the Content of this book or guarantee the reliability, accuracy, or completeness of the Content published herein and do not make any representations or warranties of any kind, express or implied, including but not limited to the implied warranties of merchantability, fitness for a particular purpose.

The Publisher and Editor shall not be liable whatsoever...

Made with ❤ on the BookLeaf Publishing Platform
www.bookleafpub.in
www.bookleafpub.com

HEAL.

Ramya Satheesh

Dedication

To all the past versions of myself who never gave up in
the face of adversity,
Who held on to faith and did the inner work to heal -
this is for you.
And to all the future versions of me,
May you always remember that we hold the power to
shape our lives,
And that a better life is always just a vibration away.

Preface

Heal - there's something so magical and uplifting about this word. It's been an ally of mine throughout life, a constant companion in times of adversity and transformation.

Healing isn't a linear path; it's a journey of constant discovery of parts hidden in crevices for many lifetimes... and bringing those parts together again, each time a little stronger, a little more whole.

This collection of poems is here to remind you that healing is always within reach, just a thought, a belief, and a vibration away. We are all sparks of the same source, and everything that flows through that source is available to us. The wisdom, the answers, the guidance - they are already here. All we need is to learn the language of our souls and trust in the process.

I invite you to read these words not just as poetry but as invitations - to reflect, to feel, and most importantly, to heal.

Acknowledgements

I'd like to thank all my mentors and spiritual teachers, without whom I could never have experienced the quantum leaps in healing that I have.

I'd also like to thank the Universe for its miraculous surprises, constantly reminding me that I am always held by a force far greater and infinitely loving.

Finally, to my husband, Vivek - thank you for being my constant pillar of strength and support, for loving me through every iteration of myself, and for listening with excitement and appreciation to every poem in this book.

The alchemy of healing

It hit me like a ton of bricks, rug swept from beneath my
feet
I gasped for air, I couldn't breathe
These things happened to others, not me
My ego whirled around looking for an ID.

My days were void, the darkness of the night competed
with the darkness in my soul
Soul? What soul?
Was this going to be the end of me?
My body and mind shriveled and dehydrated from all the
tears shed.

Grief weighed me down, making it impossible even to
reach out
To my phone, to call for help
I had no choice but to sit with it and watch it
Sometimes whispering, sometimes screaming like a baby
on a flight.

As I watched and embraced it, it began to express
I saw it melt away, clearing and making space
For what was now just a vacuum of nothingness
A nothingness of deafening silence that screamed
wisdom seeping through the cracks.

When the weeds cleared the flowers showed up
It was a rebirth, a new life
Wait a second, there are no strings attached, I'm free
I can now let the child in me out to play unrestrained.

The darkness melted into a bright new soul that was
born
Whose pain transmuted to purpose
Only gratitude for the rock bottom
Coz' when I hit it, there was no fear left anymore.

The only way from there was up
And up I rose, spreading my wings
The feathers of which were pieced together
With everything that made my soul sing.

Embracing the shadow

She was five when she first fragmented
Splintered into two frightened inner children
One took on the narrative that she wasn't good enough
Another decided to put on a brave front.

When she was nine, she fractured again
One part believed she wasn't safe
The other vowed to always be her knight in shining
armor
She had to choose one, and the second won.

When she was eighteen
One fragment told her she was unloveable
Another did everything in her power to be validated
Both existed within her, only one seen.

Now she's thirty three with multiple fragmented twins
Some shielded her and helped her survive
While others lurked in the shadows
Shunned, shamed, and exiled everytime they tried to

speak.

This brave warrior waged a quiet war
With the darkness of the fragments she had suppressed
Anger, shame, guilt, not-enoughness had no place in her
life
Their whispers for attention, to see a glimpse of light
were met with strife.

Finally the whispers became unignorable screams
She had no way out but in
In the darkness to her horror she saw
Battered and abandoned versions of herself locked up in
chains.

All they wanted was to be heard and seen
To be set free from their cage
To be given an opportunity to see the light
So that they too could go out and play.

One by one, they all came up
Anger, guilt, shame, not-enoughness
Only to be witnessed without judgment
And joined they hands with the light, giving her a sense
of wholeness.

Whispers of the Universe

The Universe is quite the chatterbox
Never shutting up if you'd listen
There's nothing it loves more than giving you answers
To the questions your soul quietly seeks from within.

Through songs and birds
And animals and words
Through numbers and synchronicity
And intuition and curiosity.

Through friends and foes
And joys and woes
Through mentors and teachers
And sometimes unsolicited preachers.

It's constantly reminding us that it has our back
We're never alone even when we are
Like a loving parent it watches over us
Gently guiding whilst allowing us our trials and errors.

Send love to this massive ball of cosmic energy
It's love language is faith and trust
Open your heart, and know you're held
And you'll be amazed at the magical delights that unfold.

Nothing but angels

The universe sends us nothing but angels
Each bearing a lesson wrapped in a life experience
Some arrive like an earthquake, shaking your very
grounds
Yet they are your compass guiding you to a new horizon
And others arrive like a warm cup of tea
Showing you that miracles and love too still bloom in
your world.

That schoolmate who bullied you
Seemed like a shadow cast too large
Yet, it was nothing but a lesson in resilience
And empathy - A fuzzy blanket you now carry
Offering a soft-landing to a world
Bruised with many an angry fists.

That dysfunctional family you were born into
That made your heart beat anxiously
And crushed the little child in you
Was nothing but a training ground

For you to find your way to your own heart
That carried the treasure of limitless overflowing love.

That broken relationship
You once believed would last forever
That felt like a knife dug deep into your back
Shattering like fragile glass at your feet
Is your lesson in letting go and being present
And recognizing patterns that show up to heal.

All the people you resent
Are nothing but messengers in disguise
Souls who agreed to step into your life
And teach you lessons that only this sacred journey
could reveal.

So listen to the message, don't shoot the messenger.
Thank them in your heart and release them with grace
Let the pain transmute to wisdom
And not be carried around like rocks in your pocket
Weighing down your heart
And bending your spine beneath their weight.

Sphere of control

Isn't it marvelous how the neutrality of an external event
Gains color and weight when passed through our mind's
eye?
The illusion of reality pulling a hood over our ability to
see
That we wield the magical power to mold our perceived
reality.

Sure the mind's a prison, and thoughts chained prisoners
But we also hold the key to unlock their chain
Freeing them to into another rebirth
Shape-shifting into another form to see the world anew.

A climb up a mountain seems daunting from the
shadowed base
But as you put one foot in front of the other and move
ahead
You'll gather presents along the way
A flicker of strength, a bloom of courage, a whiff of crisp
air and the scent of pines

Keep you engaged, until you realize you're at the
summit.

Storms may come and the earth beneath you may quake
And while you surrender to these cosmic forces
Know that your mind, your most potent tool
Holds the magic to turn every neutral event into a story,
a lesson, a blessing.

Only one of you

Look at you, darling, in all your magnificence
A once-in-a-lifetime miracle that never was and never
will be
Clutching your limitations like badges of honor
Wearing your fears like armor
Guarding yourself from unimagined possibilities.

Woven from the very fabric of source
Yet oblivious to this sacred truth
That you are the creator of your own universe
One that's as unique and magical as you.

Still, you follow the herd
Chasing goals like bleating sheep
Not pausing to see - you are the goal
The journey back to your truest self
Is the only destination worth reaching.

That crooked nose, those squinting eyes
The stretchmarks that tattoo your skin

They are signatures of your being
Never to be replicated again
For you are one of you.

So pause and savor this fleeting form
See it through your unique lens
Taste each moment as only you can
And watch as a joyous world
Unfurl its wings before you.

Deep conversations

Conversations are like adventures
No map, no guide, not sure what to expect
Sometimes a turn to a secret alley can reveal
That hidden antique shop, treasures buried
Tucked away in the depths of your subconscious
Only to be rediscovered through a fresh lens.

Questions are like roads - each revealing a new route
Taking you through different journeys
The right ones lead to the heart's open gates
Forging connections that last a lifetime
Others take you to dead ends
Where silence becomes the final word.

There's nothing more magical
Than watching a story unfold
Gently being guided by the right questions
Like hands unlocking chests covered with rusted locks
Letting forgotten truths breathe air again
Making the person feel truly seen.

So, don't shy away from the deep conversations,
The hard questions, the ones that matter.
For the words left unsaid and the questions left unasked
Can stop you from experiencing the release
The catharsis that could've been.

Rejection if redirection

Nothing hurts worse than rejection
It's like someone took a sledge hammer to your dreams
And desires and shred them into a million pieces
Dreams that you had so carefully cultivated
Thought by thought until you felt no separation from it.

When you scavenge through the shards of broken
dreams
You'll find traces of blessings
That over time show you that
The dream was never yours to begin with.
That you had picked up shoes which didn't fit
The blisters of which would've left indelible scars.

Connect the dots backwards and you'll see
That every no was making way for a more aligned yes
Unlocking a new level of refinement
Building grit, resilience, and strength.

Friendships

We speak of love, of passions aflame
Of soulmates destined in lovers' names.
But what of friendships?
The quiet force that fills the spaces
Where love alone cannot reach,
The lifeline that makes the mundane meaningful,
And without which, joy would be a solitary road.

Why do we forget to call that friend
To check in, under the guise of busy-ness
To say *"I'm thinking of you"*
To set date nights and getaways
To celebrate anniversaries of secret memories
That stay as sacred as the bond you share?

There's an incredible kind of romance
In having a 3 AM friend - your constant
The one who sees your shadows and loves you through it
Who knows your light and reflects it back at you.
With whom silences are not empty, but a comfort

Like the laughter that emanates from an uncontrollable
laughter bomb
Set off by an internal joke communicated through
meeting of eyes.

Friends are the quiet angels we often take for granted
The ones who hold us through the storms we dare not
face alone
Who hug us back home
When we lose our way.

Life can be hard no doubt
But it's always softer
With someone who checks in on you
So be that someone to the ones
Who make your heart lighter.

Set dates.
Celebrate milestones, small and large.
Treat these friendships with the same joy,
the same excitement as a new love,
And watch how your burdens shed,
How laughter and connection
Become the center of your days.

Ancestral Ties

Deep in my cells, they lay alive
All those who walked before me,
Fought wars on land and in their minds,
So I could stand here, free.

Through my pain, their sorrow speaks,
Through my beliefs, they breathe anew
The lies they told of their smallness,
Now mine to see through.
I have the power to heal these wounds,
To mend what seven generations knew.

Through me, they live the dreams they lost,
Dreams they thought could never be.
Their pain now finds a sacred worth,
As I bring it to reality.

For it's not just trauma they passed down
Their strengths run in me, too.
The wisdom of my greatest grand,

The talents her mother knew.

With every thought and every act,
I shift the tale or bind the past.
The chains that kept my kin in dark,
Unseen by the light, at last.

I meet them where the shadows fall,
Our silent exchange, a shared embrace.
Yet gently, I guide them toward the sun,
And they rise, light bathing their face.

With each breath, I honor all,
Transform their struggles into grace.
Scabs shed from wounds long healed
Because I chose to heal this space.

The art of receiving

I see you
The way you give, so effortlessly,
Pouring yourself into every space
With hands wide open, heart stretched thin.
You show up for them,
Time and time again,
But when it's your turn to receive,
You shrink, you tremble.
It feels like too much
Love, kindness, abundance
As if it wasn't made for you.
It's not that you don't want it
The warmth, the joy, the care
But something deep inside whispers
"Not yet. Not me."

You've worn the weight of selflessness,
But behind that cloak,
There's a booming echo of unworthiness.
You've mastered giving,

But receiving? That's a different language.

But hear this, love:
You too deserve.
You too are made for the miracles that surround you.
Expand your container,
let the flow of all you give come back to you.
Open the space inside where receiving feels like home,
not a trespass.

It starts with a knowing
that you are worthy of every good thing,
every soft touch of grace the Universe holds.
And when you're ready,
when even the smallest part of you whispers "Yes,"
you'll find the givers,
the ones sent to mirror back
all the love you so freely give.
When they offer you that love,
don't turn away.

Let it land in the open hands
you've spent a lifetime learning to hold.
This is the art of receiving.
It's your time.

You are so loved

Sometimes a person will come along
And crack you wide open
Tear down the sturdy walls
You've so carefully built
Brick by Brick
Shielding yourself from the storms outside.

They'll love all parts of you
The good and the bad
The dark and the light
And show you that you too are worthy
Of being unconditionally loved
Just as you are.

It can feel overwhelmingly uncomfortable
For the mind knows not about unconditional love
But the heart does
And behind those walls
It's been yearning for a place
It can feel safe, it can feel seen

And accepted with all the stitches that have been sown
To put it back together after years of heartbreak.

When this happens, just know
The Universe has seen you and has your back
It sent you an angel to love upon you
To bring you back to the knowledge
That you too are a loved, divine child
Worthy of the energy of pure, sacred love.

Ho'oponopono

I'm sorry for thinking it was all your fault,
For not seeing things from your view,
For failing to understand you were only reflecting
A hidden part of me,
Waiting to emerge from the shadows into healing light.

Please forgive me, for in a fleeting moment
I forgot that I am the creator,
The one who brought you into my life
To reveal the drama playing deep within
The recesses of my unconscious mind.

Thank you for signing the soul contract,
For agreeing to be the bearer
Of a message hard to receive,
Yet necessary for my healing and wholeness.
Through the pain you delivered,
I returned to my most vulnerable self.

I love you for the role you played,

I love you for all that you are.
You've taught me a lesson that strengthens my
foundation
A new belief, a deeper wisdom,
And a profound realization within myself.

Parents

Sometimes, we forget
That our parents, too, are just grown children,
Carrying their own burdens,
Navigating trials they never had the tools to heal from.

We forget that they did the best they could,
From the level of understanding and awareness
They had at the time.
And when they stumbled, they lacked the ability
To see their own shortcomings,
For their reality didn't allow them to.

Yet, despite their flaws, they showed up,
Doing the best they knew how,
While their inner children cried out-
Through anger, tantrums, passive aggression, and hurtful
words.
But even in those moments,
There were glimpses of the unconditional love
They carried for their children.

And here you are today,
Reading this, standing at the crossroads
Of an orchestrated journey -
Where every moment your family gave, whether painful
or loving,
Brought you here,
To become the one who heals and is healed.

Unapologetic

Don't believe the ones who say-
You're hard to love
Their words are but echoes of wounds unhealed,
A reflection of the masks they've worn
To earn a love that was never fully theirs.

Offer them grace instead.
Show them the beauty in your rawness,
In the way you claim your space with softness and fire.
For in your unapologetic truth,
You hand them the key
To free themselves from the prisons of pretended
perfection.

Be a mirror of freedom,
Where they see what it means
To exist without shrinking,
To love without losing.

This is the grace that heals

Not by changing for them,
But by daring them to become
Who they've always been.

Inner authority

When our souls were born,
They brought with them an internal GPS,
Always guiding us true
If only we'd hear its gentle whisper.

It speaks through the quiet pull of intuition,
The gnawing in your gut,
The full-body knowing,
The tides of your deepest emotions.

These are your truest authorities,
Never steering you wrong
Yet we drown their wisdom in the noise
Of families, teachers, and the world's demands.

So next time a choice awaits you,
Turn inward
For the answer has always lived within.
No one outside can know your path,
But your highest self, through these whispers, does.

Trust it, and watch how alignment unfolds,
Like a river finding its flow,
Carving your life's course with effortless grace.

No rules

Rules are manmade limitations,
Meant to control and bring order to the world,
But if they don't align with your deepest desires,
Remember - they are illusions,
As fleeting as the life we live.

Never let your heart's joys be bound
By rules crafted by those
With their own views of love, success, and wealth.
They were human, just like you,
Shaping the world from their narrow gaze.

But you-
You are limitless.
There is no stone in the Universe
Carved with the law that you cannot have
What your soul craves.

This life offers many joys,
So taste freely of its bounty.

Remember, there are no rules.
Spread your wings, let them catch the wind,
And write your own story, bold and unbound.

Forgiveness

Forgiveness is not for them, but for you,
A gentle release of the heavy stones
That weigh upon your heart,
Lowering your vibration,
Keeping the good from flowing in.

Let them go with ease and grace,
Unshackled from the chains of anger,
Resentment, and rage
They knew not the harm they caused,
For their limited sight only saw
What was right for them at the time.

Close your eyes and turn within,
Tune into the whispers of your heart.
Let go, let go, let go
Feel the burdens lift and dissolve,
As lightness seeps into your being,
Filling the void with joy and love,

Creating space for all that is meant to be.

Let go

Let go when the weight of holding on
Outweighs the fleeting comfort of connection,
When the respect you pour forth like rain
Is met with the sharp sting of condescension.

Let go when your gestures of love,
Tender offerings, are met with indifference,
When you're taken for granted,
Your soul's essence dulled by their dismissive gaze,
Forgetting the warmth of all you've given,
And counting only what you have not done.

Let go when the thought of your absence
Is a burden they can easily bear,
When they see your light as an inconvenience,
And your love becomes a shadow,
A flickering flame dimmed by neglect.

Let go when you realize
You're losing yourself in the effort to win

Someone else's heart,
Wandering in a maze of their expectations,
While your own spirit fades into the background.

Letting go is a radical act of self-love,
A declaration to the universe
That you refuse to settle for scraps,
That you deserve a feast,
Rich and abundant,
Where your worth is celebrated,
Not diminished.

So release the ties that bind you,
And heal the part within that once believed
This was all you could ever hold.

20. All we want is love

We are all so uniquely different,
Carved by the hands of our own stories,
And yet there's a golden thread, unseen,
That binds us together, heart to heart.
We feel the same emotions,
Though our triggers are worlds apart.

It's this that makes us beautifully human:
Our shared need to be seen,
To be held in the warmth of acceptance,
To be loved without condition.

The angry one, the tired one,
The one who hides behind sarcasm,
The one who always says yes when they mean no,
The one who smiles but aches inside,
The one who envies, the one who resents,
Even the one who feels nothing at all
They are all searching for the same thing.

All of us are.

We just want to be held,
To be loved for who we are,
Without masks, without pretending.

So when you meet someone
Who seems to have lost the way to love,
Take their hand with your heart.
Offer them a kind word, a gentle smile.
Remind them of the love that flows in this universe
A love so vast, so endless,
That it touches everything,
Because this world,
At its core, is only made of love and light.

And sometimes, all it takes
Is one small act of kindness
To guide them back to that truth.

The little things that matter the most

A cup of warm tea after a hard day,
Wrapping you in quiet comfort,
Like the soft embrace of an old friend.

A cozy sweater on a rainy afternoon,
Sheltering you from the storm outside,
While the world turns gentle and still.

Coming home after the longest of days,
To the familiarity of your own space,
Where the weight on your shoulders begins to dissolve.

Warm sheets on a cold night,
Like a whispering lullaby,
Reminding you that you're safe, that you're held.

A comforting word from a loving friend,
A balm for the soul, soothing the cracks
That no one else may ever see.

A random text with words of thanks,
Arriving like a gift, unwrapped and unexpected,
But filling your heart in the quietest of ways.

Puppy kisses from the neighbor's dog,
Innocent joy bursting through the mundane,
Reminding you of the sweetness in simplicity.

A cat that chooses you,
Offering affection on its own terms,
And making you feel chosen in a way that's rare.

A long drive with someone you love,
The road stretching ahead, endless and free,
With no destination, only connection.

Deep conversations with a kindred spirit,
Where words feel like rivers, flowing endlessly,
And you find yourself in the reflection of their truth.

A kind smile from a random stranger,
A reminder that even in the chaos,
There is softness and light in the world.

The brightness of a flower on a grey day,
A tiny burst of color,

A reminder that beauty still blooms even in shadow.

A familiar hug that takes you home,
To a place where everything feels right again,
Where you remember who you are.

A book with the exact words you needed,
Speaking to your soul in ways
Only the universe could have planned.

These are the moments, small and sacred,
That remind us happiness lives
In the quiet corners of the everyday,
If only we stop to notice.

www.ingramcontent.com/pod-product-compliance
Lightning Source LLC
Chambersburg PA
CBHW072050150726
47996CB00015B/2475